Fight Like a Tiger Would For Her Cubs

~ Jonathan & Martha Stone ~

Preface

This book is written to give hope, the hope that as a parent suffering from any form of mental illness, you don't have to lose to social services. You can be a survivor.

It is written to inform and reinforce the idea of hope, recovery, and a normal life for parents affected by mental illness.

The names of many people in this book have been changed to protect their privacy.

Social Services

Despite their disability, people with mental illness have normal or above average intelligence and may be highly creative. Antidiscrimination legislation is needed, to prevent social services from disrupting the lives of mental health users who want to have children and have a family.

Every child has the right to have the freedom to live with the people that love them most.

The present climate for paranoia about child abuse and mental illness is fostering a situation that promotes social engineering. Natural parents who are not abusive are being deprived of their children simply by virtue of suffering from a mental illness. Even when no allegations are made against parents suffering from any form of mental illness or if any unsubstantiated allegations are drawn up against them they stand to lose their children, and the overwhelming powers of Social Services, kick in with disastrous results in terms of psychological harm and serious trauma for those unfortunate children of falsely accused parents.

Unverified accounts of neglect or abuse are used by Social Services to the detriment of the life and development of the children, who are denied access to history and parental contact.

The Domination of the process and the System defy the principles of true justice and the rights of people. This reeks of dictatorship - individuals in departments having the power to manipulate and socially engineer young children's, and their disempowered parent's, lives.

Financial and social status seems to figure more in Social Services considerations in carers than stability in the child's prospective home. Statistics reveal that whatever the background, more children who are taken into care, result in disaffected young adults, failing in education, relationships and social behaviour.

Health visitors are often instructed to give all parents a "risk rating", if possible while the child is still in the womb, or soon after the birth - this is done without parents' knowledge or consent. The questionnaire used is highly inaccurate as a predictive tool, and has a very high rate of false positives. Anyone with a history of mental illness is on the watch list - supposedly so that they can get extra support, but it is often simply for extra surveillance. Midwives are instructed to report risk factors, and are losing the trust of the women they care for.

When social workers investigate mothers as a potential risk to their children we see incredibly high stress levels in women who fear losing their babies (even if the fear may not be justified). Research has shown this high level of stress hormones in the mother's blood can reduce the baby's growth as well as causing behavioural problems in childhood.

Expectant mothers with a history of mental illness have an increased risk of social workers taking their babies, without even giving them a chance to show that they can be good parents, and providing them support and help. The State is, in effect, saying "we are punishing you for your illness because you are a second class individual; you are unfit to be a parent".

Mothers with a previous history of mental illness (perhaps caused by bereavement or a damaging relationship), or mothers with postnatal depression (very common) or psychosis risk losing their children. The extreme shortage of mother-and-baby psychiatric units where they can safely be together is a scandal; Primary Care Trusts are seldom willing to pay for such care outside their area. The grapevine in many communities is accurately circulating the risks, so mothers who may need medical care are concealing mental illness, for fear of their children being taken. Two academic studies have shown that questionnaires to identify postnatal depression no longer work, because mothers lie. This is dangerous, since we now know that suicide is the major cause of death associated with childbirth.

Not all attempts to have children adopted succeed, and mothers may have them returned after weeks, or months. The intense bond fostered by the high levels of oxytocin the mother has from giving birth and breastfeeding has been damaged. The baby has lost the breast milk which gives lifelong health advantages, and contact visits are never frequent enough to breast feed.

"Mother with a history of mental illness has baby snatched by social workers"

She was told that her 'disability' meant their baby would be taken away from her.

Social Services have no right to take a baby away until it is proven that the parents cannot cope with the baby. Put this parallel to the case where three children were taken away because of the suspected abuse of one, which turned out to be a medical condition - they should allow this couple to bring there child up in the same way, six months with oversight, guidance and help and then if it is obvious they cannot cope it would be a different matter. Why are the father's capabilities not being looked up? Plenty of men are capable of caring for their children without a woman at their side, so why is it not appropriate for him to help bring up their child?

Social services have trampled all over several mental health parents basic human rights. The right to a marriage, the right to a happy family life, and the right to raise their child.

It should be the duty of the social services to offer whatever assistance may be needed to help parents on the road to family life, instead of passing judgement on them before they have even had the opportunity to prove themselves.

Social services are removing children because the parents have a history of mental illness, parents have a low IQ, the house is untidy, the parents are arguing or that there is no "routine" set for the children. Cases like these have been documented recently in many newspapers and on the television. No child should ever be removed from the family home unless there is evidence of severe physical abuse, sexual abuse, malnutrition, drug or alcohol dependency or severe neglect. Hearsay evidence should not be admissible in court. It is not admissible in criminal courts. When witnesses do not come to court themselves and cannot be cross examined. Statements of social workers and their experts cannot be questioned, and worse still the video's made by children under pressure to say what they are told, often contain the most outrageous exaggerations and untruths, yet they have to pass completely unchallenged in the absence of the witnesses themselves.

Once social services have decided a child should be taken into care or freed for adoption any resistance from the mother or father is considered as "non-cooperative". Social workers then use just about any means, and often go to any lengths to win their case without regard to changing circumstances or anything else but winning their case at court. If a mother has a child in care and dares to give birth again a social worker has the right to go into the hospital and immediately take the child away from its mother and family with a view to getting it adopted by strangers. This barbaric treatment is happening to mothers and families every day all over the country. After all adopters prefer babies don't they?

Parents with mental illness are the victims of stigma and societal attitudes even before they become pregnant. The normal desire to bear and raise children is undermined by negative societal attitudes. One mother said, "I guess I feel that if I got pregnant, my child would be taken away from me because I have a mental illness. I feel like I'm sterilised by the department of social services and have no rights." There is always the stigma of being mentally ill. When mothers go to the hospital to give birth, people immediately assume they cannot care for the child.

Parents with mental illness feel the additional stress of having to prove themselves. This source of stress motivates some and discourages others. "I think sometimes we make the better parents because it is so hard to be like this and we have to try twice as hard," said one mother.

Given the stigma and stereotypes accompanying mental illness, people may be quick to hold parents' mental illnesses responsible for children's problems. Even if it's normal adolescent behaviour, parents worry that the behaviour will be viewed as their fault. The assumption may be made that parents with mental illness abuse their children. A mother said, "We have a mental illness, and people think that we're going to abuse our children. We're going to take it out on them."

Mothers with mental illness may fear losing children through voluntary placements when they are hospitalised; through the involuntary removal of children when abuse or neglect is assumed, suspected, or documented; or as a consequence of divorce. Mothers may struggle to maintain relationships with children who are living with relatives or foster parents, with whom visits are sporadic or limited.

One mother said, "When you're not with them a lot, they don't see you on a regular basis, and you can't show them your love in the normal ways that mothers show their love."

Worry about potential loss may contribute to a mother's decomposition. Even when children are returned to their care, mothers may worry they will be removed again. "I think I would die if my daughter was ever taken away from me, especially for the wrong reasons—you know, incompetence," said one mother.

The termination of parental rights may have lifelong effects. One mother described these effects by saying, "My heart is in chains. It never gets easy, not for any mother; that pain never completely goes away."

Mental Illness & Parents

With nearly one in five people experiencing a mental illness at some time in their life, there is a great possibility that many of these will be parents. Some of these illnesses will only be short term, such as being depressed for a period of time following the loss of someone close, or periods of anxiety and high stress when life is particularly difficult. Long term mental illness includes such conditions as:

* Chronic depression: an overwhelming feeling of sadness and an inability to see the positive things in life

* Bipolar disorder: a condition where a person swings between feeling like they have superhuman powers and being depressed

* Schizophrenia: a breakdown in the brain's function between thinking, acting and feeling; this can make a person

think they are seeing and hearing things and cause them to withdraw socially

* Obsessive compulsive disorder: conditions where the person has uncontrolled obsessive thoughts that cause them to repeat unnecessary actions

* Chronic anxiety: a continuing feeling of being nervous, fearful and or excessively worried about events.

Having a mental illness can make parents feel very alone. When a parent is struggling with the relationships within a family, the sense of social isolation can make things even harder. Parents with mental illness may worry about losing custody of their children or feel guilty about not being able to perform as a parent in the way they want to. But it isn't all bad: with support and education, parents with mental illness can parent just as well as anyone.

Daily Difficulties

Having a mental illness can be hard work and parents with a mental illness can have a difficult time caring for children and providing them with a stable and predictable environment. Sometimes sticking to a regular routine or getting through the simplest day-to-day chores such as shopping and cooking can seem impossible. Often holding down a job is out of the question. Within the family unit, a parent may find it hard to set limits and boundaries for their children as their own judgement can often be influenced by stress or confusion.

In these situations, children often care for themselves more than they would in other situations, such as doing cooking, cleaning and shopping if there isn't enough family support. Parents with a mental illness may be unable to keep their children safe in these situations as they mightn't understand the risks their children are exposed to.

Children and Emotions

More severe mental illnesses can have severe symptoms such as seeing things that aren't really there, hearing sounds and voices and thinking that people or things are 'out to get them'. When this happens to parents, it can be very confusing and frightening for children who can't understand their parent's behaviour. Children can blame themselves and think it is their fault. They can also feel very frustrated and angry that their parent is behaving in such a way.

All the things described above can affect a child's development. The worse a mental illness is, the higher the risk to the child. Not only do parents need to be able to provide their child with food, clothing and shelter, but also teach their child about social skills, problem-solving skills, appropriate behaviour and emotional control. If a parent is struggling with these things themselves, they won't be able to be a very good role model for their child.

Sal's Story

I and my husband suffer from mental illness. I have always felt that social services would cause more harm than good. I am always fearful when they are called in. The first social worker was frightening, she used to do everything by the book without any compassion or understanding on how to bring up a child (she had no children).

We had to go to conferences to fight her decision to put our child in an "at risk register" when the child was about eight days old. We had to attend conferences involving the police, social workers, health visitors, community psychiatric nurses coupled with the added pressure of looking after a new born baby.

It felt like we were punished because of our mental ill health. The social worker implied that anyone with a mental history should not have a privilege of being a parent/bringing up their child even when there are no apparent dangers and no

concerns from the mental health professionals.

Alice's Story

I am sad while writing this because it's been over a year since social services took my daughter. It is painful to talk about what happened to me and my daughter but I can't avoid what happened because my memories won't let me forget. I keep thinking about all of the other families who are experiencing the same thing and I know in my heart I must speak out. I have to help other people who are facing this same extreme injustice and whose families were needlessly torn apart.

Annie & John's Story

What terrible crime did we commit to have been punished so cruelly by being threatened with the loss of our child? Did we hit our child? Was there sexual abuse? Was she left roaming the streets?

No. But the reasons for our brutal torment family are just as shocking. We have been judged to be "mentally ill and incapable" to have children.

The local authority ruled that the child was at risk of neglect and violence because of our mental illness.

John was criticised for becoming irritated by interference from the local authority.

Social workers who assessed us admitted that our child was loved, kept clean, well-dressed and fed-but still recommended that our child be removed because of our history.

This raises the most fundamental human question of what makes a fit parent-and do social workers have the right to make such judgements?

Our daughter was born healthy; she weighed 7lb 2oz. The baby was planned; we had been together for four years.

Annie developed post-natal psychosis following a difficult birth, and was put on anti depressants and anti psychotics to help her cope. She eventually settled down well to motherhood with help from the health visitors.

Social services got involved before the baby was born. Within three months after the baby was born, there were over seven different professionals involved.

There has been too much interfering, too many people watching us.

We cooperated with the authorities even welcoming a social worker into the family home before 7.00am and after 6.00pm.

We may not the best parents on earth, but we would try to give our daughter a good life and a good upbringing.